How to Try to Go Out

And all the reasons why you shouldn't bother

How to Try to Go Out

And all the reasons why you shouldn't bother

Elthea Marden

Copyright © 2022 by Elthea Marden

All rights reserved. No part of this book may be reproduced or used in any manner without written permission of the copyright owner except for the use of quotations in a book review.

FIRST EDITION

ISBNs
978-1-80227-717-3 (eBook)
978-1-80227-716-6 (paperback)

*Dedicated to the Lionhearts of The Ukraine,
who were forced to leave their homes in the
most brutal of circumstances.*

*Your bravery and resilience are a lesson for us
all to appreciate what we have.*

CONTENTS

Part I - Introduction 1

    Chapter 1 - The Evolution & Uprising of the Sofa 3

    Chapter 2 - Going Out Gear -v- Not Going Out Gear 7

    Chapter 3 - The Perils of Shopping & How to Avoid It 11

    Chapter 4 - Eating Out in Places & all the Reasons Not to Bother 15

    Chapter 5 - How Television Has Changed/Not Changed 19

    Chapter 6 - Transport & Why It's Best Avoided 23

Part II - All About Other People & Why They Should Be Avoided 25

    Chapter 7 - Sex & How to Have It 31

    Chapter 8 - Avoiding the Gym & Other Activities Not to Do 35

    Chapter 9 - Holidays – If You Must Go Out, Make It Matter 39

    Chapter 10 - Dog Owners Find the Bodies 43

    Chapter 11 - I've Done My Best to Teach You Everything I Know 45

INTRODUCTION

The Pesky Pandemic that started in 2019 has changed life for each and every one of us, affecting us all in different ways. 'Lockdowns' replaced 'Lock-ins,' and instead of indolently lounging around in pubs and shopping centres, we've been forced to lounge around at home instead. I believe that the hybrid state of Half-in/Half-out has suited the Great British Public more than we cared to admit. Suddenly, we have been given the excuse we've been hoping for, for years, to stop putting on our own personal one-man shows.

Once Half-in and Half-out replaced Lockdown, we began cautiously browsing in shops. The bravely vaccinated and the sceptical disbelievers came under scrutiny from little faces in pushchairs who tried in vain to understand whether these strange people were a friend or foe.

When the government restrictions lifted, we could go and do whatever we liked. The indoors, outdoors, or the outdoors, outdoors, called to us to eat microwaved ready meals from sticky, disinfected tables and choose over-priced food from sheets of wind-rattled A4 as we perched nervously at spaced-out tables. We dismissed Climate Change and embraced outdoor heaters as we shivered outdoors, 'having fun.'

Bladder capacities were extended as we learned to 'hold it,' cross-eyed with effort, rather than brave the public lavatories. On the rare occasions when it became unavoidable to avoid voiding, new lengths and levels of ingenuity, fleet of foot and flexing were all applied to pee without touching ANYTHING – even yourself. Leaving a public space became a dance of daring, offered with military exchanges in doorways. All of this guarded nonsense has become ruefully amusing less than three years into the 'New Life.' Hopefully, in a decade, it will become hilarious, and Channel 5 will make a documentary about it that you can stay in to watch.

Shopping was less fun as there was limited touching, no trying, and restrictions as to what could be taken back; I'd hate to be trying to launch a career as a Pick'n'mix salesman. It takes a hardened shopper to want to stand shoulder-to-shoulder with the germ-ridden population with whom we'd spent over a year disconnected. However, for a plucky few, flights were once more in demand as we headed out of the UK for a well-deserved, albeit tempered, break in the sun or snow.

Children returned to a semblance of normality in schools, and universities moved closer to being buildings of learning for the finer minds rather than open prisons with online learning facilities but with all the fun of mingling, sex, recreational drugs and alcohol removed. Education had taken the leap to help the younger generation reintegrate. Where did that leave the people that had a significant choice? The ones who could choose to work at home and socialise wherever they liked had a decision to make.

'Stay In' or 'Go Out'?

For many of us, though, we decided that the lure of 'fun' wasn't all we hoped for. The government had massively underestimated the British Public's desire to lie around at home doing nothing except converting calories into ... well ... more of *themselves*. So, what changed? Was it really just down to the government-imposed restrictions on our freedoms, or has this sea-change been creeping up on us all for the last decade or so?

A subtle zeitgeist has been encroaching on our way of life since the turn of the Millennium, and I think I may have the answers – it starts with SOFAs!

Chapter 1

THE EVOLUTION & UPRISING OF THE SOFA

Our parents rarely lounged on a sofa. I do not remember either one of my parents sitting with their feet raised from the floor. My parents had very limited parenting skills and had little desire to nurture or educate their children, but they always possessed the ability to remain upright when seated. Even after a full day of toiling at the joyless domestic drudgery imposed by pre-Millennial inconveniences, they would relax only by sitting upright on the sofa or in a chair.

On Sunday afternoons, they would snooze away the libations of the meat gristle from Sunday lunch by leaning their heads slightly to one side of whichever uncomfortable perch they had found for themselves.

Of course, this was largely because sofas of that generation were not created to lie upon. The arms of those old sofas and chairs were designed in two ways; right angles with minimal softness or swept in a disproportionate arc of neck-wrenching flatness that deliberately thwarted any attempt at comfort or relaxation.

Even the most louche relative could only fake a recline for the time it took to capture the image on a Polaroid, the obvious gap between body and furniture giving away the lack of comfort or support one gave to the other. An attractively acquired pose was down to core strength and sheer doggedness to capture 'relaxing.'

Upholstery was usually chosen by manufacturers based on levels of spite. The vitriolic loathing that those old upholsterers harboured was expressed by wrapping thin sponge cushions with the itchiest material they could source. Presumably, they scoured deserts for cacti variants or plantations of the most skin-irritant bushels of fibres they could find to stuff into cushions or any other furniture item that was ostensibly built for comfort.

Not only was furniture designed in a cruel way to thwart comfort, but it was also small. Sofas were largely divided into meagre, square areas with clearly defined boundaries that discouraged encroachment into neighbouring 'zones.' This clear delineation actively discouraged 'lolling' or relaxation beyond perching or something even more vulgar – snuggling.

Look at the 'Cottage Suite!' A human being could subluxate a rib on those thin, wooden, body-repellent battens of discomfort. If the wooden arms and legs didn't repel you, then surely the misery-inducing, drab, tapestry-effect cushions would have you sinking onto a bed of nails in preference. Only cats could eke comfort from them, on the condition they were placed in a warm spot and had been draped with an item of wool. Otherwise, even a desperate moggy would likely eschew such an implausible resting place.

Of course, there were TV advertisements for reclining chairs. However, they were aspirational only for the aristocracy, nascent oligarchs or technocrats who had managed to acquire a space pen and needed a reclined position to benefit from its anti-gravitational ink flow. A few chairs were fitted with a swivel action, but that was largely for effect and only served to make them more difficult to leave. Why would anyone speedily need to execute a swivel or full rotation in their own living room?

Compare those to our sofas: those bastions of luxuriant softness and bouncy cushions. No sofa is worth having that doesn't have a peninsula for leg-resting or, better still, a mechanised footrest and reclining motion.

They're also generally massive: upholstered behemoths that swamp our living areas, lording dominion over the carpets, lamps or the coffee tables of yester-year.

Leather is butter-soft and well-cushioned, complimented by back supports, in-built massagers and cup holders. God forbid that you should have to be 'lolling' on your bouncy, cosy soft cushioned day bed and need to stretch forwards to place a cup onto a table. No, no longer for us is 'reaching' an acceptable necessity. This is partly necessary due to the average sofa being so enormous that there is little space left to situate an occasional table. Many grandly titled corner units are now equipped with a cup/plate/tureen placement zone to accommodate the banquet needed to sustain us through an evening of doing absolutely nothing.

Of course, many sofas and chairs need to be 'plugged in' now too. Not in a 'Henry McMaster of South Carolina' style, but less 'death sentence' and more 'lazy bastard.' Not only is electrically powered leg support desirable in our furniture selection, but the sofa also acts as a portal to charge up a mobile device. Again, the preposterous possibility that you should have to lever yourself from the comfort of that downy sumptuousness to find an available socket is assuaged by the provision of a USB port situated in the upholstery.

Sadly, for all the comfort the modern sofa provides, most of us still require swaddling to feel entirely comfortable. Despite the heated rooms, fug of the log burner, and cuddly synthetic fibres of our sofas, many of us still need to add a blanket or bizarrely-titled 'throw.' For pre-Millennials, 'throws' happened on sports fields or rubbish dumps; now, a throw refers to a previously designated bedding item that is kept in living areas, not sleeping areas.

This ensures that the state of not being in bed can still be imitated and enjoyed out of bed, precipitating actually being in bed.

It is also a habit of a few very strange individuals to keep a throw on the bed. It apparently means that you can be middle class or aspirational thereof to have a surplus something on your bed that requires removal before you can get into it. Presumably, all that arduous adding and removing of extraneous materials and whatnots from the bed is designed to stimulate the tiredness that would otherwise be lacking, having spent the evening being torpid and tucked into the living room furniture.

Elthea Marden

When we had nowhere comfortable to sit, the lure of the plush hotel sofas and cosy pub fires beckoned us to leave the house. Since we stopped sitting on the furniture and started 'nesting' in it, the appeal of leaving it is much more of a challenge.

So, to refer to the original question, 'Why would you want to Go Out?'

Chapter 2

GOING OUT GEAR
-V-
NOT GOING OUT GEAR

So, having thoroughly examined the extreme comforts we have created by nesting into our furniture, let us now explore the impact of all this comfort on what we wear to Not Go Out.

As babies, we are dressed in soft suits with inbuilt socks for tiny feet and a little zip or buttons along the front for maximum comfort. We are then placed under cosy coverings and propped up somewhere to pass the day or simply admire our own feet. Thirst can be addressed by taking fluid in sips from a bottle with a teat. If we need to be taken out, slip-on bootees can be added, without laces, heels or buckles, of course.

Fortunately, as fully grown humans, the desire to spend the day and night in such a dormant state lessens. As healthy adults, we can slip into a 'onesie', which is *not* a baby grow because it is much larger and sometimes has pockets. If we become thirsty, we can take sips of fluid from the water bottle with the moulded sippy-cup lip on top to ensure we don't spill whilst drinking from a propped position. The onesie, designed specifically for lying down on the sofa once we have left the bed, can sometimes be converted into outdoor wear. We simply slip on Ugg Boots, footwear without heels, laces or buckles, of course.

Elthea Marden

Do you see where I'm going with this?

Undoubtedly, we must consider why we should not dress up like giant babies in the comfort of our own living rooms. We have created a cot-like zone on our sofas, with the throws/comforters, drinking from baby bottles and staring at the pretty shapes on the TV. None of this should be of any concern or alarm for our adult workforce or, indeed, society at large.

Our tastes have evolved during our enforced retreat at home into loungewear and untailored anything. Fashion was parked and left behind in 2019 pre-Covid times (PCT), and Style was replaced by Shapeless. Forget Vogue's Catwalk collection that uses terms like 'crisp,' 'edgy,' 'buttoned,' and replace them with descriptions such as 'squashy,' 'loose,' and 'elasticated.' But this might change if we have to consider Going Out.

The prospect of wearing 'proper' shoes that grip and confine our feet is not attractive, having enjoyed the luxury of padding around the house in socks or slippers for the last year or more. Heels seem like a good idea, but our calves have lengthened into a healthy lax state, and they are just not comfortable anymore. It all seems rather silly now to wobble around on a thin spike with toe-pinching edges in the guise of 'footwear!' If your feet were responsible for designing footwear with the intention of protection and efficiency, the idea of heels, straps or anything tight would frankly be outlandish and ridiculous.

If the requirement to Go Out Out demands such ludicrous and impractical impingement on our poor toes and heels, then it's probably best not to Go Out at all. Going Out has become too painful, restrictive and difficult.

Trips to the wheelie bin to dispose of all that food packaging can be managed in slippers. The new 'stiletto' is now a 'trainer' – without the complexity of addressing laces. Which of us can be bothered to bend down to do all that unravelling and doing up again?

Such comfort from our unburdened clothing is a hearty relief to our poor, confined and flatulent bodies.

However, all the comfort we have worked so hard to achieve, has come at the price of our own extra padding from weight gain.

How to Try to Go Out

If you decide you really *need* to Go Out, plodding fatly across to the wardrobe is unlikely to yield what you were hoping it might. Naturally, hours of scrolling through your phone to gawk at celebrities has probably inspired you to 'slip into something' elegant, enhancing and show-stopping as you sweep into Wetherspoons with aplomb.

The reality is that it will not be as comfortable as the slouchy, soft fabric that currently festoons your lumpy, Lockdown physique – if it fits at all, that is. Instead, your 'fancy clothes' are likely to be fitted with zips, buttons or shoulder-dislocating hooks.

If you do manage to drag the zipper to the top, accept that zips are not meant to weave and waiver their way along the garment. If they are not lying flat and straight, you probably should take off the attached attire, stay at home and wrap yourself in a throw.

Generally, buttons are fixed with cotton thread and not magic.

A huge strain on a button and its button-hole is only going to be supported for a minimal amount of time. It probably won't withstand prolonged movement – like lumbering to and from a Chinese 'all-you-can-eat' buffet. The same with seams; if every stitch is doing its job, be aware that it will only take one to collapse the whole encapsulation and leave you embarrassingly on show.

There are few clothing lines or stores that have not capitalised on this new way of lolling around at home. Whilst Ms Kardashian makes millions of dollars selling garments that apparently smooth down all the lumpy fat (for people that HAVE to GO OUT), the less glamorous outlets have focussed on loungewear that renders fat-smoothing redundant. Instead, we can drape ourselves in shapeless elasticated garments that were hitherto unheard of and happily possess the ability to stretch around us as we expand.

So let's come back to the question – 'Why do you really want to Go Out?'

Chapter 3

THE PERILS OF SHOPPING & HOW TO AVOID IT

Our biggest purchase in the lifetime of the 'Normal' is a house. Since finding ourselves spending more and more time in it, we turned to marvel at other people's property to consider in wonder how they must be enjoying/dreading their own Lockdown. Everyone's favourite trader, the estate agent, became ever so busy and exponentially raised all the property prices to make even a crappy, little flat unobtainable - unless the price reflected weeds growing out of the windows and management by a local drug cartel.

Trawling through Rightmove, all the folks that enjoyed the benefits of being squashed in together in the city now wanted not to be squashed in with other people and made a dash for everything available in the countryside or on the coast. Presumably, this was to ensure that the virus would be blown away in the wind and the waves or stay lodged in tree bark. Whatever the reasoning, houses from coast to coast were being sold at an alarming rate. I can't speak for other countries because I don't leave the house and have no idea what is happening anywhere else.

Not being allowed to drive as a means of 'Going Out' meant that house viewing could be explained away as a legitimate reason to leave your current house – I think. The rules were very sketchy about what you could do, were supposed to do, and absolutely should not do – unless there was a good reason. House shopping was a good reason.

Elthea Marden

At least viewing houses gave us a keen insight into the changing appearances of the occupants according to their own personal weight-gain/loss journey. It became an easy ice-breaker with a nonchalant 'head nod and stomach pat.'

Of course, all that Lockdown weight didn't appear from eating salads and kale smoothies.

Supermarkets have ceased to reflect the drudgery of an ordinary 'shop.' For many of us, they can provide entertainment when sauntering up and down the aisles, assessing and discussing all the milk varieties, as you balance a 70" TV on the top of the trolley.

Whilst it IS possible to access the budget supermarkets in pyjamas, some of the snobbier ones have requested that you don't attend in nightwear or without shoes. This is entirely understandable as those places have invested in lots of chilled aisles that are awash with fruit and vegetables. In the most likely event that you have forced yourself from the house in something very soft, not bothered to add a coat or anything else outdoorsy or restrictive, it is recommended to avoid the chilled areas. Instead, progress straight over to the packeted and tinned produce. It is far warmer. If you remain committed to shopping in nightwear, stick to the more welcoming shops that are less stringent on their dress code. It is the budget supermarkets that yield the most exciting goods. The Strip of Shame that runs along the middle of those budget supermarkets provides the best of European tat that caters to the needs of everything from garden birds to serial killers.

In the event that you are well-stocked on goofy items from the prolonged online shopping frenzy of Lockdown, my advice is to stay put and order your groceries delivered to your door. This will prevent the need for dressing or wearing shoes.

There are certain kinds of people who enjoy visiting DIY shops or Halfords (I was once married to such an individual – Saturdays were awful). Those people must have been joyous that the ability to browse bobbins and what-nots displayed in aggressively pedantic measurements on the shelf of googars remained open to them. What did change during the Pandemic is that those people, still dressed in trousers with pockets up and down the legs, were now accompanied by their partners and children. The reason I know this is because I was so desperate during the first Lockdown that I went into one too; a DIY store, not Halfords. Nothing short of a gun-toting posse taking pot shots at me would lure me into a Halfords.

I don't really know what Halfords sells, but I know that I have lived without it/them/those for many years. Plus, I'm yet to meet another person who starts up a conversation with 'When I was in Halfords …' I must presume that tennis players go there to stock up on something?

As a Nation of Shoppers, it would have been expected for the British Public to return to the High Street as soon as any restrictions were lifted, but it wasn't so. Confined to our homes, we did what Granny had been doing for years and started buying all manner of goofy kitchen gadgetry from the TV shopping channels. Out at work or living life, it was impossible to remain informed about electric cherry-weighing devices or automated cushion fluffers. Therefore, It was actually a huge relief to have the time to clear out a cupboard to make room for all the devices you'd been struggling without.

It was such a relief that garden centres remained open to allow us to purchase an extra shed as a place to store all the new mini/cordless/digital/automatic garden equipment we had delivered.

With all of the new tools and gadgets to get to grips with, along with the clearing of the available spaces in which to put it all, none of us had the time to Go Out. It really makes me wonder how I ever found the time to leave the house with so much to do to maintain it properly with all of the time-saving 'stuff.'

Online shopping increased exponentially because, deep down, this was what we had all been hoping for. Not the germs and despair, but the disruption of having to Go Out.

Many of us will remember a time before online shopping was available. Searching for a specific thing could literally waste hours, if not days, of our

Elthea Marden

time. It could be exhausting to trawl from one shop to another, searching out an elusive 'must-have' that had been snapped up by somebody else whose desire to 'must-having it' surpassed our own. Those days have gone. Now, with a click, it can be delivered to us within 24 hours.

So, to refer to the original question, 'Why would you want to Go Out?'

Chapter 4

EATING OUT IN PLACES & ALL THE REASONS NOT TO BOTHER

Chefs, who used to be known as 'cooks,' haven't always been celebrities with book deals and television shows. Even the offspring of chefs are skating, dancing, nose-whistling or expressing themselves on TV; such is the extent of their cooking-parent's social elevation.

Fanny Craddock was possibly the earliest media cook on television, whipping up lard-based surprises as she cajoled the audience through her pinched lips. Even with that bygone BBC clipped delivery, she was hardly a millionaire celebrity. Plus, I cannot imagine for a minute she would have gentled the torpid, mouth-breathing Lockdowners into cooking for themselves to such a high standard that they'd eschew Going Out for food.

In recent years, food has been assigned and stratified into social classifications – it's not just for eating anymore, and chefs on television have shown us what we should be doing with it. Why would we want to eat out anywhere when we've seen the light and learned how to turn food into exotic artworks? Brewer's Fayre has little appeal now with their old-fashioned servings of peas that look like … peas. The endless tuition from shouting, swearing, face-pulling, foodie fusspots has turned us into mini experts at the hob, and now we know how to turn peas into foam. FOAM!

Elthea Marden

At a time when everything was closed, most of the commercial garden centres retained a franchise of cookware. I am certain I was not alone in buying all sorts of cooking-based items out of sheer boredom and then feeling under pressure to utilise them all.

To name a few:

A pasta machine: Used once. Very messy with flying flour, time-consuming and not worth the effort.

Ceramic measuring spoons: Unused. If a spoonful of something is required, just use a spoon.

Cherry Stoners: Who am I? The Sultan of Brunei? Nibble and spit.

Bread-maker: Just what is needed by the Unmoving – hot, delicious carbs at the touch of a button.

After cooking every recipe that has ever been concocted, you can devote your life to storing it in a range of stylish plastic storage and spend the rest of the day in a frenzy of its organisation. It is not appropriate to shuffle home from the supermarket and just 'stuff' the groceries into the cupboards. They need to be arranged, re-packed and labelled in case we forget which rice is where after it has been divested from its packet and relocated into a colour-coordinated container.

If we have a messy cupboard that could make us feel like we want to Go Out, there is a television advisory programme or two that details how to decant the food to look pretty. It is no longer acceptable to retain it in its original packaging – you're not a savage! Food that you might have just transformed into a jus, foam, medallion, coulis or a tapenade will need to be arranged, and fortunately, Tidy People have been signed up by TV moguls to describe how to do it.

If, of course, you are too comfortable in your loose clothing, upside down on the furniture, and really don't care how your cornflakes are displayed (tut, tut, tut), you can simply relax. Find a television programme that describes *how* you can organise your kitchen should the devil take you, and you find you have no idea what to do.

How to Try to Go Out

Don't worry if cooking is not your thing. After all, it is a fact that every single recipe from all over the world has been cooked, adapted, improved and cooked again. Even if you have energetically displayed your lasagne into wall art, you can still bake.

There are many, many competitive baking programmes that have hopped onto the gravy train of setting one home baker against another. For some reason, we all really care that a ham-fisted farmer can do sugar work. It, undoubtedly, steals hours of our time to see this through to its gooey, iced conclusions. It is not for us to judge how this has come to be an important part of our routine, but instead, perhaps to consider why we care.

No wonder there's no time to Go Out.

Smoking at the pub used to be an added lure to an evening out. Stinky, polluting and life-limiting as it is, smoking can create a bond with fellow smokers. There was a happy time when pubs and restaurants were divided into sections for Smoking and Non-Smoking, and it seemed to be the case that the Smoking section had all the best people.

Leaving a table for a cigarette break was considered socially acceptable and often provided a welcome interlude (or even an opportunity to leg it from a bad date) to escape the tedium of a group dinner. Where it was likely that you hadn't spoken to a certain cohort of guests on an evening out, nipping out for an essential fag break could herald a sudden change in direction to meet people in the bar. Smoking provided enlightenment into all the best dinner party secrets. Having been nauseated by the happiest couple in the world that had everyone fooled, you could find yourself in the company of the smoking half of the 'happy couple' who confides between inhalations that they're filing for divorce.

I suppose now that kind of 'secret' leaks out through Facebook or the family WhatsApp group. All the fun has been removed with this new way of sharing gossip or business deals. It has removed another incentive from leaving the house or lighting up tobacco.

Elthea Marden

Aside from the fact that it stinks, kills you and others in your proximity, stains your fingers and your teeth to a colour that paint charts should call 'Curiously Disgusting,' renders your car a hostile environment and your house requiring Danger Taping from the Environment Agency, smoking does promote a camaraderie like nothing else. Old Hollywood made smoking very cool and elegant and elevated film stars into chuffing icons. Sadly, we know better now.

Many of us will remember the repulsive morning stench of clothes worn on a night out. Common practice was to dangle them out of the window to try and eradicate the smell of stale smoke. It was horrible to have long hair as that also held on grimly to the smell of cigarette smoke, and it seems disgusting now that this was considered an acceptable consequence of 'Going Out.'

When the Smoking Ban was introduced on 1 July 2007, the ruling had a significant impact on pubs and restaurants as the smoking public lost additional enticement to leave the house. Only a true addict would choose to stand alone amongst the dustbins and piles of old vomit to inhale nebulous clouds of poison.

Combined with a massive TV, supermarket deals on crates of alcohol and a comfortable sofa, there was barely any incentive to spend money to eat out or even leave the house.

Honestly – why would you bother trying to Go Out?

Chapter 5

HOW TELEVISION HAS CHANGED/NOT CHANGED

A few of us will remember when the TV was equipped with only three channels. Those three channels were mostly devoted to game shows, soap operas, sporting events and the news. When the much ballyhoo-ed Channels 4 and 5 were added, it was not the game-changer that was hoped for because we abandoned its offerings and would still persistently Go Out.

Televisions also went through a phase of being hidden in cabinets, but, of course, now, they are too massive to be hidden in anything smaller than an aircraft hangar. Most of us have been forced by the encroaching supersized Fount of Knowledge to knock down internal walls so that we can back away from the TV and house the giant sofa we purchased earlier. There are fancy wall-mounted arrangements that can be morphed into mirrors or pictures, but, however they are presented, the TV remains the sole focus of almost every living room everywhere.

The clarity of the television has grown exponentially, enabling us to see the object of our attention clearly. Heavy make-up is not sufficient to hide an enlarged pore or a slight crease, and the extra pixels delight our voyeuristic predations to spot human flaws.

With hundreds of channels bouncing from satellites to our giant TVs, we can delight in fat people becoming thinner, thin people getting fat, or fat people getting even fatter. We can see celebrities tormented by eating slugs, skating into injuries, jumping from cliffs or doing the cha-cha in a rah-rah.

Obviously, I am not going to exhaust either one of us by describing everything that can be watched on a TV because there's a good chance that one of us might miss something that we had planned to watch. The whole point is to describe the biggest changes that television has made and its even greater appeal, preventing the need or desire to leave it behind without blaring out a stream of virtual reality and information.

If you have reached the dizzy heights of watching Everything, you can watch it again, either on repeat or as a box set. Alternatively, find the programme that apparently enthrals many of us, which films people watching the programme that we have already watched or plan to watch. No wonder we don't need to go out – which of us has the time?

There are also many, many documentaries about Britney Spears. You could watch those. By the time you've got through them and thoroughly understand Britney's journey and struggles, don't despair and Go Out – there will be another one in the ether that you can download.

Apparently, as a society, we are too demanding to listen to the television without the added benefit of enhanced sound. Boombars seem to be a must-have addition, along with surround sound. I think surround sound is meant to create a feeling of cinematic excitement without the stench of popcorn and teenagers. Boombars are either driven by an inherent idleness to process regular sounds; assist the deaf; help us to become deaf; remind us that we are not deaf, or for us to live in the belief that the manufacturers think we are deaf or are aspiring to become deaf.

It must be fantastic for teenagers now as they don't need to bother leaving the house for a tiresome career fair at the local community college. Instead, they have access to multitudinous opportunities to watch behind the scenes, fly-on-the-wall programming about running an airport, police station, accident and emergency department, keeping bees, or organising a drug-smuggling operation. The world is truly at their fingertips.

With everything enhanced to the extent that the people in your living room have less clarity and interest compared with those on-screen, it is little wonder that we are hopelessly addicted to watching hours of television.

Streaming services have broadened our horizons further by showing lots of murders. Nothing is more enjoyable than nesting into the furniture, clutching a bumper packet of something with a cup of tea, whilst settling down to watch the details unfold of a gristly murder that happened to some hapless person who *did* decide to Go Out.

A genre of television that has seeped onto our screens is cosmetic surgery befores and afters. Even though most of the ones with a satisfactory result are usually streamed from the USA, they can provide a grain of hope that we too can have OUR fat sucked out, redistributed or realigned to another body part that is flatter or more lopsided than we would prefer.

If we ARE to start Going Out again, we are going to want to make a dramatic re-entrance into the world that has surely missed us, right?

It was okay to go out when we didn't get close enough to anyone else for them to see us properly behind a mask. However, if mask-wearing ceases to become mandatory and social distancing is deemed unnecessary, surgery could be our only answer. Well, of course, there isn't *just* surgery; you can have the surface of your face lasered off, injected with toxins or threads; liposuctioned fat can be added to the end of your nose, or your chin - or whatever bit of you was holding you back from Going Out. It makes sense, really, to stay at home if you haven't been able to add or subtract different bits of your body to other parts of your body.

If you spent the Lockdown looking in a mirror or at the camera on your computer, you've probably come to the conclusion that there is a LOT of work to do before you can ever Go Out again. Should you decide to remortgage your house and change your face and body into a different version of how you hoped you would look, then this will inevitably create a situation whereby you can't Go Out because you will be recovering from the surgery or procedure you've had in order for you to be able to Go Out.

Elthea Marden

It really is a Catch-22.

Apparently, general practitioners are planning strike action if they are pressured to see their patients face to face again. They will have been vaccinated, so I suspect they are equally worried about how they might look to their patients. Or perhaps the NHS is under pressure because GPs are inundated with people asking them what they can do to change the shape of something on themselves that has become confoundingly large? We will never know for sure, but evidently, medical professionals don't want to Go Out any more than the rest of us.

Full Disclaimer from the Author: *(I have never been to a careers fair, so I don't know if they normally include guidance for becoming a beekeeper or a drugs mule). If I can, I'll find out if there is a fly-on-the-wall documentary about what happens at a careers fair and try and add an addendum.*

So, to refer to the original question, 'Do You REALLY want to GO OUT?'

Chapter 6

TRANSPORT & WHY IT'S BEST AVOIDED

Going Out costs money, especially in light of the rocketing and eye-watering fuel prices. I am old enough to remember when our sofas were not so comfortable, and we were compelled to take to the streets to publicly remonstrate with the government because a litre of petrol exceeded £1.00. Those halcyon days are long gone, and if you insist on Going Out, then you should contact the Swiss Banks, instruct them to move some money around, and do it.

The glorious emptiness of trains and planes is starting to dissipate as home workers have been lured back to the offices so that less work can be done in a different space. Being the only person on the bus, especially when you're the driver, is a lost privilege as certain types of people have become determined to leave the house again.

Just in case you thought you may have been missing out by *NOT* travelling on public transport, rest assured it is still full of sniffers, pickers, spitters and starers. Should you be a picker, sniffer, spitter or starer, then ask yourself if you really need to Go Out? Staying in your own environment can be a two-way street.

Be warned. During the Pandemic, the Public were schooled in a 'new' word: 'unprecedented.' The Pandemic became the great excuse, the Get of Jail Free card, that vindicated lousy customer services everywhere.

Long queues, lack of availability, low stocks or generally 'piss-poor' service were explained away with a wave of the apathetic hand and the blame firmly placed at the door of the humble germ.

Germs are the invisible little rascals that have terrified, modified and stupefied every experience we may have tried to enjoy.

You can't even sit in A&E for a while now with an 'itchy something' because 'Due To An Unprecedented Demand,' itches are no longer part of the service.

Before the 'unprecedented times,' you could expect a beverage thrown into the ludicrously over-priced hair salon visit. Forget that now. Hairdressers have cottoned on to the idea that tea and coffee making eats into their profits. Therefore, they've harnessed the 'unprecedented' times to do your colour, interrogate you regarding your 'Going Out' plans and holidays, whilst all the time, refusing you a drink. Or a magazine – too germy.

I think after the years of living with COVID-19, nothing should be 'unprecedented' now. It's been precedented for enough time for all the poorly-designed, understaffed, faulty, undercooked, or just plain crap to have been ironed out and streamlined into something that might tempt us into trying to Go Out.

A heads up to those who haven't been out in a while, you still can't smoke indoors in a public place, so if setting fire to leaves is your thing, stay in.

Part II

ALL ABOUT OTHER PEOPLE & WHY THEY SHOULD BE AVOIDED

'It's not that I dislike people … … … … … … … … … …

I'm just bored by their petty problems,
Appalled by their personal habits,
Critical of their life choices,
Dismayed by their noise,
Underwhelmed by their sporting achievements,
Repelled by their stupidity,
Disgruntled by their apathy towards self-improvement,
Horrified by their clothes,
Repulsed by their smells, secretions and emissions

… … … … … … … … … But I wouldn't say I dislike them.'

People are everywhere, and if you are to resume Going Out, you are bound to meet up with them. Queueing at a distance has helped in shopping scenarios, and masks are a God-send as a disguise or defence against participating in conversations, but our ears are still vulnerable. If we start Going Out again, being subjected to drivel and whining is inevitable and can ruin an otherwise perfectly happy time.

This is what I was referring to when I listed petty problems. Being isolated at home, sometimes with our 'loved ones,' made us take stock of what is truly important to us. Hours of footage showing ventilators and death, relieved only by happier shots of wore-torn, poverty-stricken, hopeless despair, have provided a new perspective on what a 'problem' looks like. Feeling cross about one of the teachers at your child's school because she doesn't appreciate what a gifted child you have, pales into tiresome persiflage and gum flapping.

Just a note to parents, no one has EVER been interested in what your child is/was/has done/doing unless they happen to have either done/been doing it on your property/to your child or you.

Author's Disclaimer: Most of our problems are petty unless we are facing mortal danger. I probably should not minimise them in this way, but I am trying to write a light-hearted account of why you shouldn't bother Going Outside. If you find yourself in a downward spiral because of what you've read, you probably *should* Go Out – for Counselling, a big bag of chips and peas, or whatever support will help.

Now, on to sport. Some of it can be mildly engaging but allow me to explain why we should remain underwhelmed by sporting achievements. It is not that I encourage being self-centred, but I don't know how to respond.

Let us consider the apparent achievement of Emma Raducanu (someone of whom I had remained happily ignorant until I went 'Out' and talked to people.) Whatever she had achieved was talked about everywhere! What are we supposed to do with that information?

It must be a marvellous feeling for her that, having spent her life perfecting her ability to hit a ball with a bat, she has become quite the savant. This lifetime of ball-hitting with a bat has culminated in her proving that she is slightly better than someone else who has also spent *their* life perfecting their ability to hit a ball with a bat. No wonder she is jubilant.

I am quite certain that she lies in bed at night, pinching herself with glee that she proved that she was better than someone else who had devoted their life to ball-hitting with a bat. I feel a small pang for her that, having devoted her life to such an action, she has now peaked too early and will need to find something else, equally pointless, to do. It is nice for her that she's kept herself fit.

I am not bitter about her achievements but rather bored and baffled by them. As such, the confusion leaves me wracked with hand-wringing hopelessness about how to pretend to celebrate them. Whilst I have singled out 'bat-wielding,' I am equally disaffected by most other sports-related activities.

Friends posted on social media accounts comments such as 'Wow! What an ACHIEVEMENT! Fantastic News – She's Done it.' Instantly, the pressure is on me to respond out of an *esprit de corps*, but for the life of me, I can't figure out what to write. I remain truly baffled about how it affects anyone other than the bat-wielding/swimming/running/kicking/flicking Who's-it who has managed to propel something or someone somewhere for no reason other than to pass the time and embarrass the rest of us because we have been at work and unable to concentrate on such nonsense.

Just on the off-chance that there are others out there feeling the same way, it is clear to me that we should be avoiding speaking to other people. The pressure to care about a flash-in-the-pan sporting event is far too stressful for anyone who has been isolated for a prolonged period, and such exposure is going to be a setback.

In case Emma Raducanu is reading this (and I am certain she will), I should clarify that I do know that tennis is played with a racquet and not a bat. I used the term 'bat and ball' in an attempt to level up her achievements with the rest of us who struggle to do up zips and buttons.

I stand by everything else.

Personal Habits and Why They Are Revolting

The personal habits of others are trying if not plain abhorrent. Masks have helped us here and, therefore, should remain mandatory, especially in cars, houses, or anywhere that there is anyone else. Masks should be mandatory for ALL van drivers to prevent nose picking whilst driving to minimise nausea and vomiting in others. In the absence of a mask, burkas are recommended.

Anyone who has ever lived or worked alongside another human will be able to recall a time when the other person was suffering from a cough. The sound of someone else's coughing is a revolting surprise for the ears and the eyes. Even if there is a warning of 'I'm going to cough,' it doesn't lessen the blow of the auditory and visual assault of the germ-spreading coughing. A sentence that nobody has ever said is, 'I love the sound of other people coughing when I'm trying to do something.'

On two separate occasions, I flew 5,500 miles for a holiday with someone who, along with their clothes, packed a cough. If the sound of the coughing wasn't bad enough, then the resultant moan following the cough, followed by the verbalised reasoning as to where they could have 'caught' the cough, not to mention all the other times in their past when they had experienced a similar cough, was enough to have me spending the entire holiday drunk on Pink Panthers to dull my senses. This cough also cost me money because I got so drunk to minimise my annoyance at the Cougher, I was robbed without realising, and I completely blame the Cougher.

Anything on the inside of a human's body is there for a reason. Leave it be. If something needs to come out, then it will, and we've become extremely clever at creating the appropriate place for it. If there is anything else, there is no need to fetch it, share it, look at it or show it to anyone else unless medically directed to do so.

If you Go Out, there is a horrible chance you might end up being close to someone who does not have the same reservations about sharing what's inside them by introducing it to the outside of them.

Covid can only be described as a blessing to ward off those people. It is not only the Author that finds such over-sharing of excretions, secretions and emissions undesirable. When the government orders directions on how to keep such expulsions to yourself by sneezing or coughing into your own elbows via national television campaigns, we can all understand that a problem exists.

How to Try to Go Out

A question we must ask is, 'WHO was sneezing and coughing over other people until they were directed to stop?' Unless these individuals can be identified, I believe there is a very good reason to avoid ever Going Out again.

Chapter 7

SEX & HOW TO HAVE IT

Now look, I want to manage your expectations; this is not a self-help book or a manual of any kind. There was a recognition that I mustn't try to omit sex from the reasons not to Go Out. Sex can obviously be enjoyed 'in' (and 'in and out' - pardon the pun), but generally, you need someone else with whom to have the sex – in or out.

As sex is one of the strongest drivers of human behaviour, tapping into a source is going to be high on the list of priorities that make leaving the house a necessity – or so you would think.

Sex is the reason that men and women end up sitting at tables in restaurants, staring past each other with nothing to say. Once the sex has stopped, you are left with the drudgery or starry-eyed pleasure of finding yourself stuck or happily attached to that one person, day in, day out, for the rest of your life. The rest of your whole life until it is snuffed out into oblivion. It's a sort of sex tax/benefit.

Teenagers used to sit in dark corners of pubs and clubs, driven mad by the incessant pounding of loud music, biting at one another's necks until their dads turned up to bring them home. If the slip of paper with a scrawled number lasted the trip, the neck bruising, and the lack of transport, then sex could happen.

This tactical coordination required significant investments of effort, time and money. Washing (fingers crossed) and grooming, in case of being lucky enough to enjoy a late-night rattling of the bins behind the kebab house, took much preparation, often transport and a voluntary home evacuation.

Even when sofas were uncomfortable and not draped in furry nesting materials, Morrissey lamented and complained bitterly about the effort it took to find a sex partner, and he *must* have been able to afford a large television.

Finding your best outfit to invite maximum allure, with matching shoes, should be placed in the hands of experts and not left to amateurs such as you or I. The competition out there is pretty stiff – with all the standards having been set from the TV whilst you were tucked up in synthetic fibres and dust from the second tube of Pringles on the corner unit.

Don't be hard on yourself – the frame of reference you see on the television was most likely recorded prior to the Big Lockdown, and the players were surrounded by a team of experts. They were also paid to leave the house. This is in stark contrast to you, who might have to pay hard cash in order to do any activity outside of the house close to what you've just watched on the TV.

Many years prior, perfume or aftershave used to be a requirement because meeting people in person meant that they could smell you. Long Covid has potentially decimated the manufacturers of *pong* because so many of the population, most likely the ones who insisted on Going Out, have had their olfactory senses corrupted into everything smelling of burning or everything smelling of not smelling of anything. Anyone remaining unaffected by this blight has a cause for celebration when travelling anywhere, buying anything or visiting anyone.

You may need to add this to your long list of reasons why you shouldn't bother leaving the house. However, if the lure of sex still seems worth it, then smelling of something other than your bed will need to be factored into the costs and effort.

Luckily, most dating is now confined to the internet. Tinder on a tablet enables users to find their potential mate and life love whilst tucked up in their nest with nothing groomed and watching The Tinder Swindler on Netflix. It is a modern miracle that every stage of a human-to-human relationship can be enjoyed from the point of introduction right through to an embittered and mutually vitriolic ending without either party having met the other.

How to Try to Go Out

It is my firm belief that this is due to the continued and unsustainable electronic contact. Such un-intimate travails in finding The One promotes a new and largely uncelebrated level of 'safe sex.' Absolutely no protection is required, except for the exposure to abysmal grammar, incomprehensible abbreviations and ridiculous emojis that have replaced communication on a grand scale.

This still leaves you, nestled into the furniture, comfortable enough to be considered bed-bound but not actually in bed, and yet thoroughly sex-less.

Are you weighing up the options as to whether it can be worth leaving the house?

The Author is of an age where there only used to be two types of sex – 'normal' and homosexual. Women had not used to be included in this because only men could choose properly as women hadn't yet been instructed on what they might like.

Fortunately, the world has evolved to include a panoply of sexuality and has become a far more interesting and diverse landscape to explore the possibilities. It may even be considered exciting enough to tempt some plucky people to Go Out.

Like most things, I believe you can pay for this sort of service, although the Author remains unsure whether or not this is legal and, as such, denies any recommendations either way. Due to my lacking any knowledge or experience other than that gleaned from watching the television, the responsibility is placed in your hands should this be something you'd like to explore and/or rent/purchase.

Having read this far into the book, it is understandable that you may be teetering on thinking it may just be worth a sneaky trip Outside. You don't have to commit to the idea but might leave just to check whether or not it is as bad as you might have imagined. I must stress that it is a personal choice. The responsibility, should you have decided to wear clothes that fit, with uncomfortable shoes, to spend the evening with someone on whom you should probably have swiped left, lies entirely upon your shoulders.

Elthea Marden

Note from the Author: *The only things I have ever hired on a temporary basis are mini diggers, skips, a carpet cleaner (which provided equivocal results), and a Welsh Cob called Cyril for a week's trekking. Therefore, no recommendations or responsibilities will be made nor offered to the reader. Any forays into the above are entirely at the reader's own risk.*

Chapter 8

AVOIDING THE GYM & OTHER ACTIVITIES NOT TO DO

I think, by now, you understand the many reasons why you *shouldn't* venture Out but let's stay optimistic and consider our increasing options. There is no need to get dressed because, before you consider leaving the house, it is important to thoroughly research where and how you will get to where you think you might like to visit. It is reckless and time-wasting to simply leave the house without thoroughly scouring and scrolling through the internet and social media platforms to see what other people have done before so you can do it too. This, in turn, will provide you with an opportunity to post a picture of yourself 'enjoying' whatever it is that someone has previously claimed to enjoy. It is usually important, once you have made a similar commitment, to prove that you enjoyed it more and wore a far more stylish or improbable outfit that increased the level of pleasure.

From my research, I have concluded that there is very little reason to leave the house, even if you are driven by your own motivation or that of the tiresome Dr Michael Mosley, to take exercise.

My personal favourite is Leslie Sansone, who has made a career out of teaching people how to walk at home. Clearly a woman after my own heart, the irrepressible Leslie has recorded not just one informative visual that gives instructions on how to walk – at home – but too many to count. All the recordings are called 'Walk At Home,' which sounds simple. However, Leslie, shadowed by a team of copycat recruits, has delivered hundreds of these recordings: a clear indicator that after watching, there was a large cohort of people who just didn't get it.

Having watched and subsequently followed along with quite a few of the videos, Leslie reminds us throughout to 'Walk, walk, walk' - in case there is a want of understanding as to why we have tuned in. It is truly baffling that she has had to re-record and deliver the instructions. We really have embraced an all-encompassing, paternalistic approach to life.

Even during the period of having small and uncomfortable seating arrangements in the home, church attendance was starting to dwindle. It is hardly surprising when taking into consideration how uncomfortable it is to sit on a pew.

Assessment of risk versus benefit in terms of leaving the house to worship whilst exposing yourself to a potentially life-threatening illness is unlikely to yield an outcome of high church attendance. If the rock-hard pew-sitting doesn't deter a congregation, then surely the close proximity of a cemetery will clinch the deal?

I am not a religious expert, so I cannot comment on the comfort or non-comfort of other houses of worship; however, it seems to be a common belief that God is always with us. If that is not granting permission to not Go Out, I really don't know what is.

Social Media is very supportive of trying to get you Out. We must appreciate the irony of needing to understand in detail what we could be letting ourselves in for by going somewhere, to immerse ourselves in research at home before we even try.

It is best to confine yourself at home, on your gigantic sofa, to thoroughly research things to do out of the house whilst still firmly ensconced in it!

The Author did some careful research on such enticements listed on Facebook Groups to understand the levels of temptation out there. Amongst the offerings of ghost walks (?), themed walking tours minus the threat of spirit companions, and classic tractor pulling days, one group that piqued my interest was a 'Potential Fencing Club' with a current membership of one.

The Potential Fencing Club was to be held at a Village Hall in a remote part of the United Kingdom and detailed that no 'proper' equipment was necessary.

This led me to imagine that the member would be seated alone in the said Village Hall, complete with a saucepan-cum-helmet, possibly with a net curtain to complete the Look, wielding a bean cane or a poker with a cork on the end. Whilst there is only my imagination to reconcile this, it didn't make me want to leave the house to find out.

For anyone interested in ice-skating, then you WILL need to Go Out to achieve a semblance of competence. It seems that global warming may be reducing the probability of naturally occurring slippery surfaces that you could use for practice. Therefore, heading Out to a local ice rink will become necessary in order to nail that triple Lutz or the Salchow.

(Full disclosure from the Author – due to a realistic fear of slippery surfaces, my frame of reference is limited to information gleaned from the internet and television. No responsibility for misinformation will be assumed by the Author.)

After YEARS of research, the Author has discovered that *some* people go to the gym. Quite why that is, I am still trying to find out. It seems curious to me that some people are so determined to fight nature and Go Out specifically to lift heavy things – that they could lift at home; run artificially – that they could do at home; grunt and puff – that they could do literally anywhere (even though I'd rather they didn't) in order to have a shower (?), put different clothes on and go home, apparently pleased with themselves. There is a membership fee to do this, which costs real money that these people give TO the gym – a racketeering enterprise if ever there was such a thing!

Whilst I felt I should include the option, I didn't believe that anyone reasonable would consider such an improbable way to pass the time outside

Elthea Marden

of their own homes. However, I felt pressured to deliver a balanced appraisal. Unfortunately, I am unable to add any further clarification on this activity because of the lack of personal knowledge, interest or tangible belief that it really happens.

Chapter 9

HOLIDAYS – IF YOU MUST GO OUT, MAKE IT MATTER

I truly believe that if you really are determined to Go Out, then you may as well make it a Big One and Go Out for a week, or even two, if you think the cat or the children will be alright to be left for that long.

Whilst the whole point of the book is designed to help you avoid the need or desire to leave the house, there is no reason not to have a holiday and stay in, in another country.

Once home working or hybrid home working became normal, it became very awkward to work out when you were at work and when you were at home or on holiday.

The Staycation became the phrase on everyone's lips which sounded like it belonged in this book. It does not. The term 'Staycation' hints at tents in a muddy field five miles from your home. Whilst I applaud the tenacity and fortitude of people wishing to quell the tide of climate change by never going anywhere, I cannot bring myself to endure or recommend a holiday as a 'rough sleeper.'

I can almost get on board with wanting to spend holidays in a static caravan; they have large sofas, televisions, and food that can be stored and eaten without moving far. Plus, they are seemingly welcoming to people dressed in nightclothes during the daytime. Despite the fact that they tend to be eye-wateringly expensive and slightly reminiscent of a Russian Gulag, they do cater for a population that doesn't really like Going Out. Caravan parks have spent years of research and resources into building an enclave where a home-from-home, with bingo and chips as an add-on, can be enjoyed for a week or two without the need to invest in any major changes to your wardrobe, diet or exercise regimes.

If you really need to Go Out somewhere for longer than a day and don't want to travel too far or leave the country, then a caravan might be the answer. Slowly towing your own home on wheels is a smaller option, but this cannot really be considered as Going Out – you are simply towing your 'Inside' 'Outside' and possibly staying in somewhere of slight difference.

Try not to be too concerned if the Lockdown has granted you the gift of becoming a larger version of the person you used to be. This is of benefit to everyone who liked you prior to there being even more of you. Should you have concerns that your swimwear might be a little on the tight side, rest assured that it will stretch. And, if left long enough at the bottom of the wardrobe, it will possess the tensile strength of dental floss – creating that extra 'give.' Obviously, you couldn't wear this locally, but in another country, it will be perfectly satisfactory because no one will know you to report back on any fabric splitting accidents.

Before you embrace the excitement of going on holiday, there is much more preparation than there used to be in the good old days of travelling with an old biscuit tin full of Penguin bars, an airline ticket and a sombrero. 'Paperwork' is now needed to escape this home for another. The rules have relaxed a little, but there is a risk that the Hungarian form you completed online will be demanded by the airline staff, at speed, in an electronic format. The whip-like presentation of each document requires such mental alacrity, administrative skills and application that it becomes advisable to be accompanied by representatives of the FDA and the Department of Homeland Security. They will hopefully get you as far as the departure gate.

Airports have spent years being a lot less fun than they used to be. Many of us can still remember a time when you could take sandwiches on to a flight without them being considered a potential explosion risk. Forget personal grooming, too, as everything you may use, like a comb or some toothpaste, is highly likely to be confiscated by over-zealous security guards.

I find it quite flattering that airport security officials imagine that I might be sufficiently knowledgeable, athletic and possess the skills to transform a lipstick and half a packet of cheese and onion crisps into some kind of weapon that could bring down an aeroplane. At home, I struggle to retain socks that match, have anything that can light a candle, unblock a sink, lift almost anything, or sit down in a chair without groaning. Therefore, it feels somewhat nice to be considered potentially dangerous and a generalised threat to International Security, rather like James Bond.

Of course, there are some ways to make your own fun before heading through the panicky chaos that is airport security. When being searched with the beeping wand thing, or being patted down, make intense eye contact with the security guard, grin constantly and make little 'hmmm' noises. Remember to thank them sincerely afterwards and with an awkwardly long hug. Then leg it as rapidly as possible into the Duty Free in case they actually enjoyed it too.

I thoroughly recommend packing any unwanted toiletries that have been gifted by your travelling partner. Prepare for mock outrage and faux displays of disappointment as they are speedily confiscated into a bin – two birds with one stone, I say.

Mask wearing is ubiquitous and expected, if not mandatory, on public transport, but there are advantages. It is no longer embarrassing to fall asleep, drooling from a slack jaw and snoring because masks hide your obnoxiousness. Of course, they don't quite cover up the head-jolting pig snort, but they go a long way to disguising it and make identification much more difficult.

People used to dress well for a flight, hoping to make a 'good impression' when landing on foreign soil. That has stopped now, and most flyers look cosily dressed, as though they have just tumbled straight from their sofa and rolled right onto the plane. There is little shame as adults, already dressed in pyjamas or the closest thing to pyjamas and giant fluffy socks, clutch a pillow from their own bed to keep them nested in their seats, whatever the duration of the flight.

If you belong to the smug, fully vaccinated against Covid cohort, you can skip through country borders like a happy lamb without putting anything (non-recreationally) up your nose. Sweating for 48 hours after a PCR test and wondering whether you'll have to go into paid confinement really took the fun out of going anywhere for any reason. Fortunately, only the needle-phobic, belligerent hippies that fuss about having 'choices' have to do this now.

(This information was correct at the time of writing, and you should ALWAYS check the entry requirements of the country or place you intend to visit. The Author also doesn't advocate putting things up your nose unless medically directed and particularly not before travelling. This may even apply to the smugly vaccinated).

Chapter 10

DOG OWNERS FIND THE BODIES

Pets are charming additions to the home and will happily nest into the sofa amongst the crumb-based detritus of the home-working, Netflix-watching population. Those furry little rascals have a way of inveigling themselves into every aspect of your life – and changing it to suit them.

If you have a dog, you understand that it will need, if not demand, to Go Out. Walking the dog has few off days (unless you are blessed with a rare, lazy dog). Of course, there are dog walkers who are more determined to leave their houses and can be employed for a reasonable fee.

Even on the worst weather days, it is always the dog walkers who are braving the gales, lashing rain or chest-deep snow to walk their beloved pets. I am not always convinced that dogs don't feel it is *their* duty to walk their owners – such is the owner's dedication to leaving the house.

If there is a body to be found, it will usually be the grim discovery of a dog-walker. Few dog owners are gifted with finding money or treasure because our furry friends love the smell of decaying anything. The scent of money is far too fresh for their disgusting radar to identify.

Any news coverage following the discovery of a body will almost certainly include an interview with the dog-walker who made the discovery. He (or she) will be hovering at the edge of the car park, clutching a small bag of shit and bristling with a barely-suppressed air of purpose and excitement. Your local news may even attempt an interview with the dog.

Once you have accepted the task of daily walking, you will have committed to leaving the house. Fortunately, you may not have to go far or even get changed out of your onesie or lounging attire; dogs don't mind. Clever coordination can combine the dog walk with a supermarket trip, post office chore or anything else that may force you from the nest. It should be stressed that this can only happen if your pooch is entirely secure because the last thing you will need is to lose them to some scoundrel or to have to chase after your fleet-footed pet for any reason.

In answer to the earlier question of 'Why would you want to Go Out?' having a dog is a key driver and should be carefully considered if you're on the cusp.

A happy compromise is a cat. Cats, too, are gifted with assuming leadership over their owners – or is it cats that end up having to deal with their humans? It's never been clear. Any cat owner will have stories about how their moggy will dictate feeding regimens, waking-up times, bedtimes and visitor-leaving times. If you have never owned a cat, you are probably smugly assuming that you would never be so idiotic as to allow a mere feline to write the house rules.

I can't help you.

So, this is probably the only plausible reason I can think of for Going Out.

Chapter 11

I'VE DONE MY BEST TO TEACH YOU EVERYTHING I KNOW

I promised myself and my readers that I would offer a balanced view of the world, post-Covid, in order to entice all of you to Go Out again. I lied. I couldn't do it and feel quite ashamed that I waited until the very last chapter to admit as much. I blame it largely on Lockdown, the extreme comfort of my own sofa and all the options to entertain myself by not leaving the house.

Descriptions of what was still out there are primarily based on hearsay, television reporting, past experiences and my own imagination. I did admit to not going to a gym, which is entirely true and baffling to me that anyone would. I used to do it before the Pandemic, but now I just pay the membership fee – an arrangement that seems to suit me *and* the gym.

In the interests of complete honesty, I have not personally embraced man-made fibres but fully appreciate their popularity and suitability for rolling around on the sofa. I can testify to the loss of elasticity to be had from swimwear if left unused for a few months.

Dressed like a baby in loosely fitted clothes, tucked up and entertained, there is little in the way of appeal to tempt you Out of the house – unless it is into the house of another. Food, sex or a home-based emergency seem to be the strongest motivators, so my best advice is to stock up on one, hope and

Elthea Marden

plan for the other and keep your fingers crossed that one won't happen. (You can decide which action belongs to which motivation).

Enjoy your home and all it has to offer. You can even watch the tennis and let me know why you found the experience exhilarating. I really would love to know, and who knows, I may even see you at Wimbledon (or is it Wombledon? I'm never sure).

Happy Staying In, and Long May it Continue.

www.ingramcontent.com/pod-product-compliance
Lightning Source LLC
Chambersburg PA
CBHW012009090526
44590CB00026B/3941